ROCK CLIMBING

ADVENTURE SPORTS

ROCK CLIMBING

SCOTT WURDINGER & LESLIE RAPPARLIE

CREATIVE EDUCATION

Published by Creative Education
123 South Broad Street, Mankato, Minnesota 56001
Creative Education is an imprint of the The Creative
Company

Design and production by Blue Design
(www.bluedes.com)
Art direction by Rita Marshall

Photographs by Alamy (Agence Images, Michael Clark,
Tariq Dajani, Ed Darack / Darack.com, david sanger
photography, david hancock, iconsight, ImageState, Jon
Arnold Images, Ladi Kirn, Andrew Kornylak, Jef Maion
/ Nomads'Land – www.maion.com, Chris McLannan,
Brad Mitchell, The Photolibray Wales, david sanger, Jan
Stromme, Stock Connection, StockShot, Jack Sullivan,
Weldon Thomson, John G. Wibanks, WoodyStock, xela)

Printed in the United States of America

Library of Congress Cataloging-in-Publication Data

Wurdinger, Scott D.
Rock climbing / by Scott Wurdinger and Leslie Rapparlie.
p. cm. — (Adventure sports)
Includes bibliographical references and index.
ISBN-13 : 978-1-58341-394-4
1. Rock climbing—Juvenile literature. I. Wurdinger, Scott D.
II. Adventure sports (Mankato, Minn.)

GV200.2.W87 2006
796.52'23—dc22   2005051785

First edition

9 8 7 6 5 4 3 2 1

ROCK CLIMBING

Heart pounding, hands sweating, legs shaking ever so slightly, a climber approaches a jagged rock wall looming menacingly above the uneven ground. Taking a deep breath, she places her hands on the cold rock. Its surface is scratchy and rough, but that is good since it will provide friction for the soles of her rock shoes. Slowly, methodically, she begins to climb, concentrating on each handhold and every little nub of rock protruding out from the face. Soon, she falls into a steady rhythm: grab with an arm, pull, place a foot, push, grab with an arm, pull, place a foot, push. Her sweaty palms make the rock wall feel slippery and difficult to grab. The higher she climbs, the harder her heart pounds. The rope connecting the climber to her belayer has enough strength to hold the weight of a car, but clinging to the side of a cliff 60 feet (18 m) above the ground is unnerving.

Adrenaline defines the adventure sport of rock climbing. Strenuous physical activity and mind-numbing mental challenges—where one wrong move could lead to a fall—make this sport simultaneously risky and thrilling for rock climbers of all skill levels.

Even though rock climbing carries a certain element of danger, the precautions a smart climber takes will make for a climb that's relatively safe. A climbing rope that will hold a major fall is one of the most critical pieces of equipment.

How much farther to the top? The climber glances up anxiously, but only for a second; she doesn't want to lose her grip. Summoning all of her strength, she pushes upward. Finally, her hand reaches over the edge of the cliff. She takes her last step and finds herself once again on flat ground. Exhausted, her arms and legs aching, the climber gazes at the beautiful scenery that stretches endlessly before her. She smiles wildly; she has done it!

Emotions such as elation and success bring climbers back to the rock time and time again. The triumph of ascending a monstrous rock face, the exhilaration of scaling an artificial wall, the rush of scrambling from boulder to boulder—rock climbers thrive on the heart-pounding thrills of this extreme sport. Requiring fitness, balance, mental acuity, and—perhaps most of all—courage, rock climbing tests the limits of even the most seasoned adventurer.

Grasping a small thrust of rock face, an experienced climber knows how to shift his or her body weight and maximize arm and leg strength in order to move to a secure handhold. Gripping rock and moving cautiously takes both physical energy and mental patience.

The First Climbs

The first people to climb mountains did so for strictly practical purposes: to hunt, to travel from one location to another, or to fight an enemy. In the 18th century, however, people began to climb mountains for sport, pushing themselves to be the first to reach a mountain's summit. Early mountain climbers didn't have much in the way of safety equipment, so they risked climbing vertical rock only when absolutely necessary. Less than 100 years later, some climbers decided that the challenge of summiting mountains wasn't enough; these were the first rock climbers.

One of the first climbers to attempt to scale vertical rock in America was Scottish-born adventurer George Anderson, who was drawn to the grand peaks of California's Yosemite Valley. Anderson was determined to be the first climber to reach the summit of Half Dome, an intimidating 8,842-foot (2,695 m) peak. To climb the rugged mountain, Anderson pounded large bolts into the rock, creating footholds for himself. Each day, Anderson scaled the bolts he had already secured and added new ones above them. Historians estimate that it took Anderson a month to install all of the bolts, but in the fall of 1875, this tedious process finally resulted in success when Anderson met his goal of becoming the first person to summit the mountain. Although Anderson's method of inserting permanent bolts into the rock is

The tools and gear that assist rock climbers have developed and changed rapidly over the last 100 years. Today, high-tech materials such as aluminum alloy make tools and gear lighter than ever before, easing a climber's burden and improving safety.

not considered environmentally sound or aesthetically pleasing today, it helped to pave the way for future rock climbing pioneers.

By the end of the 19th century, more and more climbers were seeking the challenge of scaling vertical rock faces. In Wyoming, Americans William Rogers and William Ripley devised a plan to scale Devils Tower, a spectacular mass of rock that looks as though it erupted from below Earth's surface and immediately solidified into a series of irregular columns. In 1893, Rogers and Ripley built a 350-foot (107 m) wooden ladder, the backside of which was covered with a series of sharp pegs that they drove into a crack on the southeast side of the rock. The ladder brought Rogers almost halfway up the 865-foot (264 m) rock face. Scrambling the rest of the way to the summit, he proudly planted an American flag.

The desire to find the ultimate climbing challenge leads many rock climbers to the base of Mount Everest, part of the Himalayan mountain range in Asia. Many climbers spend months attempting to reach the summit of this imposing mountain.

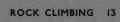

Climbers continued to utilize permanent bolts and ladders on climbs around the United States into the early 20th century. Then, brothers Joe and Paul Stettner transformed the sport. The two men, who had immigrated to the U.S. from Germany in 1927, began to use climbing equipment from their home country. With **pitons** and carabiners from Munich and a rope from a local hardware store, the two men made the first ascent of the 1,675-foot (510 m) east face of Longs Peak in the Rocky Mountains of Colorado. After their successful climb, climbing enthusiasts across North America began to use pitons—which slip into cracks in the rock—and ropes to climb rock directly, instead of scaling ladders and other hardware attached to its surface.

In the 1960s, the sport made another leap forward when American climber Yvon Chouinard created and used **nuts** and **hexcentric chocks** to climb. Although these devices are inserted into cracks in the rock much like pitons, they can be removed more easily and leave no scars on the rock. Today, rock climbers continue to use such equipment to scale higher and harder routes.

Rock climbers worldwide travel to scale the slopes of Cerro Pissis, the third-highest peak in the Andes mountain range and all of the western hemisphere. This rocky mountainside has long made for lengthy adventure climbing expeditions.

Tools of The Climb

Clinging to the side of a sheer rock face high above the ground goes against every natural human instinct. Balanced precariously on a tiny nub of rock, it is hard to forget that one wrong move could spell disaster. Fortunately for rock climbers, a number of safety devices have been developed to minimize the risk of slipping and to protect climbers in the case of a fall.

One of a climber's most important pieces of equipment is the climbing rope, which is designed to catch him or her in a fall. The most common rock climbing rope is 10.5 millimeters (0.4 in.) thick and comes in 200-foot (60 m) pieces. Although kernmantle climbing ropes are incredibly strong, they can withstand only a specific number of falls. For instance, a three-leader fall rope can withstand three significant falls from the lead climber without breaking. However, after the third fall, the rope must be retired since another fall on it could have deadly consequences.

As they climb, lead climbers place protection, also called pieces, into tiny cracks and spaces in the rock. These small pieces of equipment, which are typically made of lightweight aluminum alloy, serve to anchor the climbing rope and to support the climber's weight in the event of a fall. Non-mechanical forms of protection—such as nuts, hexcentrics, and tricams—range in size from a bottle-top to a softball. One end of the

protection is tapered, allowing a climber to insert it into a crack in the rock. By yanking the protection downward, the climber wedges it securely into the crack. **Friends** and **cams** are mechanical forms of protection that, with the push of a lever, can be reduced from their original size to fit into a crack. Once a mechanical piece is inserted into the crack, the lever is released, allowing the piece to expand to perfectly fit the opening.

Carabiners—pear or "D"-shaped clips with a one-way, spring-loaded gate—are used by climbers to attach the climbing rope to the protection. A carabiner is clipped to the metal loop on the protection, and a climbing rope is pushed through the gate of the carabiner, which will not open when weight is placed on the rope. The lightweight aluminum of a carabiner can typically hold 4,000 to 6,000 pounds (1,815–2,720 kg) with the gate closed, enabling it to support the weight and force of a falling climber.

It isn't only what they climb with that protects climbers; what they wear is important, too. A helmet protects a climber's head from falling rock, one of the most dangerous and unpredictable components of climbing on natural rock faces. Made of hard plastic, helmets also increase a climber's chance of surviving a serious fall.

Climbers also wear climbing harnesses, which consist of leg loops and a waist belt, to which the climbing rope is attached. The belt and loops are sewn together with heavy, industrial-strength thread. Harnesses are often padded to prevent circulation from becoming restricted when a climber falls or is lowered to the ground.

Most climbers wear rock shoes, which are specifically designed for scaling vertical rock faces. The sticky rubber soles of these shoes provide friction, keeping the climber's foot secure against small footholds and flat surfaces of the rock. Since they are extremely lightweight, rock shoes do not weigh climbers down as they attempt difficult routes.

The modern, lightweight, aluminum carabiner that is used by climbers was created during World War II and has its origins in the steel carabiners that are used in the sailing industry to secure ropes. Today, carabiners come in a wide variety of shapes and colors.

The Way To The Top

Standing on his toes, a climber stretches as high as he can, attempting to reach the next handhold. The tension in the rope slackens as his belayer anticipates his next move. The climber knows what he has to do to keep going. Bracing himself, he pushes off of his secure footholds and jumps upward, praying he won't miss his target. Reaching out, he feels the cold, scratchy rock beneath his left hand. His arm muscles ache as his body swings from side to side; he quickly locates two footholds to minimize the motion. He did it—what felt like a leap for life. Taking a deep breath, he continues upward.

Of course, only the most experienced climbers would ever jump to reach a handhold. For most climbers, the rule of thumb is to maintain three points of contact with the rock at all times. Thus, climbers typically move only one foot or hand at a time, finding the next foothold or handhold and moving whichever appendage will provide the most stability. Proficient climbers use the biggest muscles on the body—the legs—to move upward. They rely on their arms only for difficult moves, such as reaching around an overhang or jumping to reach a hold, since relying too heavily on the arms is extremely fatiguing and may result in a failed attempt.

Rock climbing requires the participation of almost every muscle in the body in order to sustain and complete a climb. In addition to honing their abilities on rock faces, many climbers also spend time lifting weights to increase strength and flexibility.

California's Sierra Nevada is the highest mountain range in the continental U.S. To reach climbing areas, backcountry hiking and camping may be required. Most climbers find that the thrill of reaching a summit in this region makes the journey worthwhile.

As climbers move up a route, they continually examine the rock above them to find the next handhold or foothold. Every hold looks different: some are large outcroppings of rock; others are small nubs barely visible from the ground. In fact, sometimes there are no holds at all, and climbers must rely on their rock shoes to help them stick to the wall or employ a technique called flagging—which involves placing the foot against a flat section of rock and using it for balance, rather than for support, until a sufficient foothold can be found.

As they search for hand- and footholds, climbers must also carefully keep track of their route. Failing to do so could lead to a route that is below or beyond their skill level. Accidentally ascending an easier route may prove dissatisfying, while a more difficult route could be perilous.

Lucy Creamer (below) is one of the world's leading rock climbing experts. She began climbing at the age of 10 and today travels in search of new, challenging routes. Her favorite climbs are in the United Kingdom (UK), her native country.

Kinds of Climbs

A climber hikes up a steep mountain path, ropes wrapped around her torso, carabiners and other hardware swinging at her sides. She moves carefully up the steep slope. At the top, she glances around and moves to the edge of the cliff, looking over to see her friend below. She has found the top of the route they want to climb. Quickly, she uncoils a rope and lays out the hardware. Tying the rope around two trees, which serve as anchors, she sets up what looks like a slingshot. With two carabiners, she attaches the middle of a second rope to the middle of the first, then throws both ends of the second rope over the cliff. She walks back down the path to the bottom of the route where her friend is waiting. Their day of top rope climbing is about to begin.

Top rope climbing is the safest way to gain experience in rock climbing, since the climber is securely anchored to the top of the route. Once an anchor system is set up, both the climber and the belayer clip into the rope at the bottom of the route. As the climber ascends, the belayer takes up the slack in the rope. If the climber starts to fall at any time during the climb, the belayer catches him or her through the friction of a belay device, which holds the slack rope and prevents it from running back through the carabiners clipped to the anchor rope. Once the climber reaches the top,

Many climbs involve a strenuous hike to the base of the rock face before the climb can even begin. Climbs in such rugged terrain demand a high level of physical fitness, as simply carrying ropes and other gear on these hikes can be exhausting.

the belayer lowers him or her to the ground by letting the rope slide through the belay device in a controlled manner.

The risky technique of lead climbing is much more challenging than top rope climbing since there are no solid anchor points to catch a climber during the beginning of a climb. In a lead climb, the lead climber first free climbs part way up the rock wall and inserts a piece of protection into a crack, which serves as the first anchor point. The climber then connects a carabiner to the protection and the rope to the carabiner. The rope runs from the lead climber through the carabiner and down to the second climber at the base of the rock, who serves as the belayer. As the lead climber continues up the route, he or she places protection wherever possible. The more often the leader can place protection, the better, since in a fall, the climber will drop twice the distance from the last piece of protection before the rope catches him or her. Once the lead climber reaches the top, the climbers switch roles and the lead climber becomes the belayer from the top of the rock. As the second climber moves upward, he or she removes the protection left behind by the leader. Eventually, the second climber reaches the top, having removed all of the protection, effectively leaving the rock face "untouched" by human use. To return to the ground, climbers often rappel down the rock.

In multi-pitch climbs, which can be hundreds of feet long, climbers often take turns as the lead climber. Since the lead climber must place pieces of protection into the rock with one hand while holding on to the rock with the other, lead climbing requires an incredible amount of exertion. The second climber in multi-pitch climbs can rest periodically by serving as the belayer while sitting or standing on a small ledge or rocky outcropping on the way up. This way, he or she will have the energy to lead the next pitch.

Top rope and lead climbing on natural rock are known as "trad climbing," or traditional climbing. Traditional climbing was the only way to climb until the late 1980s, when sport climbing was introduced. Although sport

Free climbing is more dangerous than top rope climbing, but it is the most common form of ascent. Crack climbing (left) is a form of free climbing in which climbers use only their fingers and feet—no tools—to inch their way up a crack in a rock face.

Bouldering is a unique climbing form that tests one's strength and ability. The U.S., UK, and France all feature distinguished bouldering problems and climbs. Often, exceptional bouldering can be found close to difficult rock climbing routes.

climbing is much like traditional lead climbing, sport climbers do not insert protection into cracks in the rock. Instead, they use **quick draws** to clip their rope to a series of bolts that have been securely drilled into the rock face. This form of climbing is not the most environmentally friendly, but it is a great way to test out skills before attempting the more challenging lead climbing. Sport climbing also allows climbers to ascend rock faces that have no cracks, since the bolts are actually drilled into the rock.

In addition to traditional and sport climbing, many people have begun to climb indoors on artificial walls. These plastic, wood, or fiberglass **resin** structures provide climbers of all skill levels with an opportunity to climb year-round or to train for just a couple of hours. Some rock walls are very simple, consisting of a cement block or planks of wood with small, oddly shaped handholds bolted to the wall in various patterns. Other artificial walls strikingly resemble natural rock features, with bulges, cracks, and **chimneys** strewn across their faces. Usually, these look-a-likes also have plastic or fiberglass resin handholds bolted to the surface.

An alternative to climbing rock faces is bouldering. As the name suggests, bouldering involves scaling boulders, which are typically only about 10 to 15 feet (3–4.5 m) high. Boulder routes, called problems, can include treks up, down, or across a boulder. Bouldering is considered by many to be the purest form of climbing since it does not require the use of any equipment other than a pair of rock shoes if the climber desires. Because climbers are rarely very high off the ground, a rope to catch a falling climber is unnecessary. Many boulderers do, however, place a thick pad on the ground to cushion their landing in case of a fall.

Rating Systems

A wall of red granite rises from the rocky ground. Even from its base, hand- and footholds are obvious, jutting out from the rock face at dramatic angles. Several beginning climbers mill at the bottom of the wall, awaiting their turn to place hand to rock. Just a few yards away, another wall rises. A lone climber clings to one of its many sections of overhanging rock, his belayer concentrating intently on his every move.

With rock walls of varying difficulty levels scattered throughout the world, everyone from novices to experts can find a climb to suit their abilities. In many places, easy rock climbing routes can be found near difficult routes. In order to help climbers determine whether or not they are qualified to attempt a particular route, rock climbs in North America are rated according to three different classifications: grade, class, and seriousness. Climbers can refer to guidebooks to learn the ratings of specific routes.

Grade refers to the amount of time it will take an average climber to complete the route, which allows climbers to judge their level of commitment to the climb. Grade levels are denoted with Roman numerals, with I the easiest grade and VII the most difficult. A Grade I climb takes approximately one to three hours to complete. Grade II climbs usually require two to four hours, while Grade III climbs can take up to six hours. A full day is needed to scale a

Grade IV route. Climbs rated Grade V through VII often require a climber to spend one or more nights on a ledge high up on the face of the rock. These climbs should be attempted by only expert climbers who can handle varying weather conditions, unexpected emergencies, and complex climbing. Although grade is a good reference point for the time required to complete a climb, it is relative to a climber's level of expertise. Expert climbers may be able to complete a Grade VI climb in a single day, while the same route could take an intermediate climber many attempts and days.

Class refers to the difficulty of the climbing route; ratings range from hiking trails (Class 1) to vertical climbs that require a rope (Class 5). Class 2 and 3 climbs, while a bit steeper than Class 1 climbs, do not require a rope,

Rating systems describe the severity of a climb. Many difficult climbs, such as the Arawata Crag in New Zealand (below), require climbers to receive a permit. This ensures that only appropriately experienced climbers try scaling the rock.

since a slip on such terrain will not become a fall from a height. Class 4 climbs, although not necessarily vertical, usually require a rope since a slip or fall could cause serious injury. Belays and anchor points are required on Class 5 climbs, which also demand careful selection of hand- and footholds.

Class 5 climbs are further subdivided into classes 5.0 (easiest) through 5.14 (most difficult). Ratings for Class 5 climbs are always determined by the most difficult move on the climb. For instance, a multi-pitch climb may consist mostly of 5.5 moves, but if there is one 5.10 move on the route, it will be rated 5.10. Moreover, a lowercase letter following the decimal rating further breaks down the difficulty of a Class 5.14 climb. For example, a 5.14a is easier than a 5.14c. Class 5 is an open-ended rating, and as more difficult climbs are found, lowercase letters continue to be added to the rating scale. As of 2005, the most difficult routes found on natural rock walls were rated 5.14d.

Seriousness consists of a three-point scale that describes how easily protection can be placed throughout a climb. Guidebooks usually use "R" and "X" ratings to alert climbers to dangers when lead climbing. If a climb does not have a seriousness rating of R or X, a climber can assume that the climb offers many places where protection can be inserted into the rock by a competent leader. On the other hand, an R rating means that protection may be either difficult to place or insecure once placed, and the leader may risk a lengthy fall. If a climb carries an X rating, it means that places for protection are lacking, and the lead climber will be unprotected for long sections of the climb. A fall could result in a fatal injury. Most climbers avoid R- and X-rated climbs because of the extreme risks they present.

Today, bouldering has become so popular that it has its own rating system. To rate bouldering problems, North America uses the "V" system, invented by John "the Verm" Sherman, one of the pioneers of modern bouldering. The V system rates a problem from V0 to V14, with a higher number representing more difficulty. A V0 problem is roughly equivalent to a 5.9 vertical route, while a V14 is as difficult as the most extreme vertical climbs.

Around 1890, early pioneers began rock climbing in the Peak District of the UK. More than 10,000 rated climbs are now found in the Peak District National Park. Many well-known climbers, such as Lucy Creamer and John Arran (opposite), enjoy the parks' climbing challenges.

Hit The Rock

American climber A. Alvarez sums up the experience of climbing: "On those rare occasions when mood, fitness, and rock all come together and everything goes perfectly, you experience an extraordinary combination of elation. As calm-tension dissolves, movement becomes effortless, and every risk is under control—it is a kind of inner silence like that of the mountains themselves."

Of course, before a beginning climber can experience this sense of elation, he or she has to learn how to climb effectively. The best—and safest—way to learn to climb is to participate in a rock climbing course. Organizations and guide services throughout North America offer introductory to advanced climbing classes. Although it helps to be located near natural rock climbing areas, many indoor climbing facilities provide instruction as well. It is important to keep in mind, however, that the instruction received from an indoor facility is quite different from the instruction required to climb natural rock. Although indoor and outdoor climbing utilize the same techniques, climbing on natural rock also requires a knowledge of how to set up ropes and use equipment.

Organizations such as Outward Bound, National Outdoor Leadership School, and Eastern Mountain Sports offer indoor and outdoor climbing courses throughout the world.

Before clipping into carabiners on natural rock climbs, many climbers build up their confidence, strength, and skill level on indoor rock walls. Becoming proficient with climbing equipment, however, usually means gaining experience on natural rock.

Rock formations located throughout the world give climbers a chance to become acquainted with the native terrain in an unusual way. From ocean cliffs in Thailand (left) to mountains in South America, great rock climbing can be found on every continent.

In addition, a number of smaller rock climbing schools are located near many mountain ranges. These organizations offer comprehensive rock climbing instruction that provides climbers with in-depth information about fitness, clothing, equipment, and safety techniques. Rock climbing schools often offer a range of courses, from half-day seminars to month-long programs. In addition, some organizations provide individual courses. These courses are more expensive than group courses, but are generally more efficient since the instruction is focused and intensive.

Of course, just because a person knows all there is to know about rock climbing does not mean that he or she has developed the skills needed to climb rock. Most rock climbing courses focus on learning through doing, allowing students to gain experience by actually climbing. This gives students an opportunity to receive immediate feedback on their technique.

Once climbers have mastered the blending of skill and knowledge, they can turn their sights to the great climbs of the world. Some of the better-known climbs in North America stretch through the Rocky Mountains and into the Sierra Nevada mountain range of the western U.S. Joshua Tree National Park in southern California, known as "J Tree" to frequent climbers, offers more than 4,500 climbing routes. Surrounded by desert, this climbing location provides a unique experience for both beginning and expert climbers.

Farther north, in central California, Yosemite National Park is home to El Capitan, the largest monolith in North America. Known as "The Big Stone" to climbers worldwide, this extreme rock rises more than 3,000 feet (915 m) above the floor of the Yosemite Valley and takes an average of four days to climb. Its more than 70 climbing routes boast colorful names such as Realm of the Flying Monkeys, Lurking Fear, and Lost World.

Grand Teton National Park in northwestern Wyoming hosts millions of visitors each year. Climbers from around the world are drawn to the 13,770-foot (4,200 m) Grand Teton, the highest peak in the Teton Range.

Today, a climber on the Grand Teton Mountain in Wyoming can still ascend to the spot where members of the Rocky Mountain Club—who were the first documented climbers to reach the summit—drilled a piton into a boulder.

Devil's Tower in Wyoming is a giant stone thrust that lures thousands of climbers from around the world every year. Cracks in the face of the tower supply climbers with numerous paths, with ratings that range from 5.7 to 5.13.

With more than 35 routes of varying difficulty levels, this spectacular mountain is accessible to novices, experts, and everyone in between.

The West isn't the only place to climb in the U.S. In the East, West Virginia's New River Gorge provides more than 1,400 climbs in the Appalachian Mountains. Most of the climbs are rated 5.9 or higher, however, so this area is best left to advanced and expert climbers. The Red River Gorge in nearby Kentucky offers more than 1,200 routes for climbers of all skill levels. Both the New River Gorge and the Red River Gorge offer extraordinary scenery—meandering rivers and lush hardwood forests—and the chance to interact with climbers who have come from all over North America to test the rock.

Although not home to any mountain ranges, the Midwest also offers several climbing areas. The most extensive, Devil's Lake State Park in southern Wisconsin, features more than 1,600 routes, rated from 5.1 to 5.13a. The 30- to 90-foot (9–27 m) cliffs around Devil's Lake consist mainly of smooth quartzite, providing climbers with a unique challenge. For those interested in staying close to the ground, the area also offers several bouldering problems.

Southwestern Utah boasts some of the most diverse rock climbing in the U.S. More than 1,500 climbing routes are located in as few as 50 acres (20 ha), or 20 square city blocks. This variety draws numerous adventure climbers and backpackers every year.

CompeTiTions and FesTivals

Rock climbers who develop a passion for the sport and attain a rare level of skill may choose to climb competitively. Many athletes thrive on the adrenaline rush of facing off against two challenges: the rock face and rival climbers.

Two climbers approach a 40-foot (12 m) artificial rock wall, checking their harnesses and ropes. Everything seems secure. They nod to each other and turn to concentrate on the wall. On a mark, they begin to climb, looking as if they are running up the wall's vertical face. Suddenly, cheers erupt from the crowd below; Olena Ryepko of the Ukraine has just won the women's speed climbing competition at the 2005 World Climbing Championships.

Ryepko was one of 300 of the world's top climbers who descended on Munich, Germany, for the World Championships in 2005. Like many competitions, this event featured races in three categories: speed, lead, and bouldering. Speed competitions test a climber's ability to quickly scale a climbing route, as competitors race two at a time up parallel climbing routes. After scaling the wall once, the competitors switch routes, and their total time is used to determine the winner. Joining Ryepko—whose total time was 38.07 seconds—as a gold-medalist at the 2005 World Cup, Russian Evgeny Vaitsekhovsky won the men's speed competition with a total time of 20.39 seconds.

Climbers in lead competitions—also called difficulty competitions—focus on technical climbing prowess rather than sheer climbing speed. Climbers in these competitions must move deliberately, nearly contorting their bodies to reach awkwardly placed hand- and footholds on a 50- to 130-foot-high (15–40 m) artificial wall that features many sections of overhanging rock. Routes in lead competitions are so extreme that often climbers don't reach the top. In such cases, whoever reached the highest point on the route is declared the winner. Nineteen-year-old Angela Eiter of Austria took the gold in the women's lead competition at the 2005 World Championships, climbing almost 100 feet (30 m) up the rock face, 20 feet (6 m) higher than second-place finisher 19-year-old Emily Harrington of the U.S. In the men's competition, three climbers reached the top, so the winner was determined based on results in the semi-final round, earning Tomás Mrázek of the Czech Republic the gold.

Even though personal strength, determination, and a love of the outdoors push climbers to their goals, many agree that without support from their fellow climbers through climbing clubs, competitions, and festivals, the sport would not be as rewarding.

In bouldering competitions, climbers attempt several boulder problems—all at a maximum height of 13 feet (4 m). The climber who reaches the top of the greatest number of problems in the least number of attempts wins the event. Olha Shalagina of the Ukraine mastered all six boulder problems at the 2005 World Championships on her first attempt to take the gold in the women's event, while Salavat Rakhmetov of Russia also solved all six problems on his first attempt to place first in the men's competition.

Both competitive and recreational rock climbers can learn more about the sport and meet others who share their passion for rocks at climbing festivals throughout North America. Many of these festivals not only celebrate the sport, but also raise money and awareness for various causes. The Red Rock Rendezvous, held in Red Rock Canyon, Nevada, for example, raises money for the Access Fund, a national organization that works to keep climbing areas open. The three-day event, held every March, features clinics by climbing experts, demonstrations of the latest climbing gear, competitions, and service projects to benefit the local environment.

The HERA (Health, Empowerment, Research, and Advocacy) Climb for Life in Salt Lake City, Utah, raises money for ovarian cancer research through donations, registration fees, and sponsorships. This multi-day event drew more than 200 participants in 2004 and had the support of more than 40 climbing sponsors. Since its inception, satellite HERA events have occurred in Las Vegas, West Virginia, British Columbia, and Wyoming.

Canada also hosts several rock climbing festivals each year. The more popular festivals, such as Granite Fest in May and Rocktoberfest in October, occur near the city of Montreal River Harbour on Lake Superior in Ontario and are sponsored by the North of Superior Climbing Company. These festivals last for several days and include training clinics and product demonstrations.

Today, whether it is a large competition, a well-known festival, or a few friends having a day of fun, it's a sure bet that wherever there are rocks, there will be rock climbers trying to meet their insatiable desire for adventure. The spread of rock climbing competitions and festivals across North America, along with the surge in the construction of indoor climbing gyms, continues to bring the sport to more people in more places. At the same time, improvements in rock climbing equipment are enabling individuals to climb more complex and challenging routes. As the sport continues to advance, one thing is certain: the thirst to reach the top will always drive thrill-seekers to the rock.

RECOMMENDED READING

Jackenthal, Stefani, and Joe Glickman. *The Complete Idiot's Guide to Rock Climbing*. New York: Alpha Books, 2000.

Long, John. *Gym Climb!* Helena, Mont.: Falcon, 1999.

Ralston, Aron. *Between a Rock and a Hard Place*. New York: Atria Books, 2004.

Toula, Tim. *Rock 'N' Road: An Atlas of North American Climbing Areas*. Guileford, Conn.: Globe Pequot Press, 2002.

Watts, Phillip Baxter. *Rock Climbing*. Champaign, Ill.: Human Kinetics, 1996.

WEB SITES OF INTEREST

www.bigwalls.net/climb
Offers an in-depth look at climbing gear, as well as photos of various climbs.

www.icc-info.org
Describes climbing competition rules and lists the results of several climbing competitions.

www.indoorclimbing.com
Lists indoor rock climbing gyms around the world and provides information on indoor climbing competitions.

www.northofsuperiorclimbing.com
Describes climbing courses and events sponsored by the North of Superior guide service.

www.peakfinder.com
Provides historical information and descriptions of various peaks across North America.

www.rock-climbing.ws
Describes the different types of climbing used in different venues and the various rating systems for rock climbing routes.

www.uiaa.ch/index.aspx
Offers information on the International Mountaineering and Climbing Federation, the organization that oversees many climbing competitions around the world.

www.usaclimbing.org
Provides information on the U.S. National Climbing Team, with competition results, newsletters, and sponsors.

GLOSSARY

aluminum alloy—a metal consisting of a combination of aluminum and another metal or two forms of aluminum

belay device—a friction device through which the climbing rope passes; it allows the belayer to manipulate the rope and catch a climber in the event of a fall

belayer—a person who pulls the slack out of a climbing rope as another climber ascends; taking up the slack rope is a safety precaution called belaying

cams—mechanical pieces of protection that are removable and reusable; a cam consists of two, three, or four disks mounted on an axle; pulling on the axle causes the disks to spread apart to fit a crack

chimneys—wide cracks with parallel walls into which a climber can fit

free climbs—climbing without a rope or protection of any sort

Friends—brand name of one of the original kinds of cams; today, many climbers refer to any brand of cam as a "friend"

hexcentric chocks—non-mechanical pieces of protection that are removable and reusable; a hexcentric chock consists of a six-sided nut attached to a wire loop

kernmantle—a type of rope that has a twisted core (kern) with a braided sheath (mantle) wrapped around it for protection

lead climber—the first climber up a route; the lead climber places protection as he or she climbs

monolith—a large block of stone that stands alone

multi-pitch—a long climb (usually longer than the length of a climbing rope) with multiple ledges along the way, from which the lead climber can stop and belay a second climber

nuts—non-mechanical pieces of protection that are removable and reusable; a nut consists of a metal wedge attached to a wire loop

pitch—one length of a multi-pitch climb; often the length of a rope or the length to the first substantial ledge

pitons—pieces of non-removable protection that are placed into cracks on a rock face

quick draws—short, strong pieces of nylon webbing with carabiners on each end

rappel—descend a vertical wall by sliding down a rope in a controlled manner

resin—a man-made solid or semi-solid substance that is often white or yellow in color

scrambling—the act of climbing using the hands, knees, and body; this type of climbing does not require a rope

tricams—non-mechanical pieces of protection that are removable and reusable; a tricam consists of a single disk with a point that can be wedged into a crack

INDEX